The

Sue MacIntyre

The Wind Today

Hearing Eye

Published by Hearing Eye 2010

Hearing Eye, Box 1, 99 Torriano Avenue
London NW5 2RX, UK
email: hearing_eye@torriano.org
for book orders: books@hearingeye.org
www.hearingeye.org

ISBN: 978-1-905082-61-2

Acknowledgements: Earlier versions of several of these poems were published in
Picnic with Seafog and Elephants (The Many Press, 2003). A number have
appeared in these magazines and anthologies: *Artemis, Brand,
The Interpreter's House, Scintilla, Second Light Newsletter,
The Stony Thursday Book, Parents* (Enitharmon/Second Light, 2000),
In the Company of Poets (Hearing Eye, 2003), and
Images of Women (Arrowhead Press/Second Light, 2006).

—〰—

My warmest thanks to Jane Duran and Mimi Khalvati for their help and
encouragement during the preparation of this collection; to Susan Johns and
Karen Green for all their editorial help and advice; and to Martin Parker for his
design skills and patience. Many thanks, too, to the Thursday Group and to the
Advanced Poetry Workshop for their comments and suggestions.
Sue MacIntyre

—〰—

Hearing Eye is represented by
Inpress Ltd in the UK – see www.inpressbooks.co.uk
Trade distribution: Central Books, Hackney Wick, London E9 5LN

Printed and bound by Imprintdigital.net
Designed by Martin Parker at www.silbercow.co.uk
Cover image: from woodblock print 'A Sudden Gust of Wind at Ejiri'
by Katsushika Hokusai

Contents

for David,
Dan and Helen

Waterfall, 1911

Each face is a distant thumbprint
   with its own nameless whorls and dots.
The nursemaids are the thumbprints with shady hats,
   the women with high-piled hair are family,

their men in shirtsleeves and waistcoats,
   elbows on the grass, one standing tall, heron-like,
teacup handle in the fingers of one hand,
   saucer resting on the other.

Out of this blur, my small mother
   hunched on the grass
curls round and peers at me. My aunt,
   smothered in white robes and bonnet,

lies in her frowning mother's arms
   among her family of strangers
from the Mill House and the Valley Hotel.
   And behind them the waterfall – shining,

sending its spray into the orchard branches
   as the smiling tribe drink their tea
staring at me, transient on their
   fragile raft of rugs and grass.

Strawberries

Odette's footman is bringing in the lamps.
It's a winter afternoon, outside

the low dark street,
the careless disarray of the season,

but in this small space the lamps read
like embroidered strawberries

in a dusty tapestry. She has plumped up
her great cushions of Japanese silk

for Swann, keeping a sharp eye on the footman,
scolding him for his clumsiness.

There's a harsh scent of chrysanthemums.
I don't want to move forward

or back, but stay, until the scene,
the scents breathe off the page –

it's like coming upon my great-uncle's
brown wallet in a box of stale family papers,

unfolding it and finding
his wife's two small wills inside;

she thought she was dying twice.
Her white hair and giggle float up.

She writes to 'My darling husband'
in her precise ornate hand,

apologises for her silly ways,
lists her bequests – to me

her seed-pearl bird brooch,
her turquoise earrings.

Shutters

The handed-down degrees of darkness
traditional in these stone farmhouses,
permutations for blocking out the light:

the casement opens inwards, a dark
brown shutter hinged on it. You can lock
the shutter to the casement with small

coarse blocks of wood, then hook
the darkened window half open and
half shut – spillage of light at top,

at bottom, shield from heat or bats,
or in early morning unhook and swing
the whole thing open, fold both sides

back against the wall, rest on the sill,
loll there, breathing white mist and
the beginning of sun. Or lock it all out,

seal the heat and light away –
the lock's called *spagnoletta*, a black rod
the length of the window frame and

a handle. The frames groove tightly,
one turn and you're in darkness on
an iron bed, afraid you'll not remember

the rush of mountain water, pinkish stones,
the quick evening closing of the sun,
movement of goats in the valley below.

Sunflower Harvest

This time I came to the valley in September.
It was filled with another crop, the crop
of the total eclipse of the moon,
the machines going heavily at night

under bright lights, harvesting tobacco.
And the sunflowers? Before,
the land was splashed with their yellow,
irradiating huge spaces, opening doors,

their erect heads anxiously turned
to stare at the sun. Now they are crumpled,
brown as bats, necks bent, small heads
down, such a spillage of self, such a shrinking.

I felt they were you: when you came
to the door your face showed more than grief,
your world out of joint, as if a harvest was
nothing more than a spilled seed basket.

Waking Elegy

A hand is sliding the dolls forward slowly
out of sleep. They begin to take their places

on the windowsill. The pawns are moved up
into the sunrise and slowly I remember

there are gaps on the chess table that can't be filled,
moves that can never be made again.

Opening myself to the sounds of the ivy garden
where the rustle of squirrels muffles

the terracotta armies in the earth
and distant birds sing of God's election plan

and the lost embroidered routes,
I try to hold back a while longer, to stay hidden,

not yet move into the world of 'and then'
where a boy at a desk is still

doing his word puzzle, making loops
around the letters word by word.

Walking Away

for Marisa Berna

Breath of mist in the early morning,
    white scarf of mist in the valley,

and today, a bank of white,
    leaving only the dark outlines

of pines and broom near us
    as if they're on the edge of a precipice.

You're moving away from us
    in the beginning of sun, followed by

the big dog and the small dog,
    on your daily walk, carrying a small basket.

For a moment you become three silhouettes
    against the white, then disappear.

Where will you come back?
    What edge, what border will recreate you –

your brown face, your strong step,
    your attendant jogging animals?

Visitation

You are shy, you are goatlike,
    you come in early morning,

light eyes curious, head
    heavy with a budding horn.

Not a whiff of farmyard,
    musky scent of whiteness,

nesting for a moment
    near my pillow's whiteness,

bringing with you a sense
    that sets dreams reeling,

that enlightenment and eternity
    have white curly hair on their skins.

You trail the scent of countries
    where people have never been.

You trot in to graze at my pillow
    and leave a bag of milk at my head.

A Wineglass Half-full of Milk

When I came out of the dream
where you were drying the soil of a pot plant
with a hairdryer, and slowly climbed
to the kitchen, you had already left.
Beside the cooker was a wineglass half-full of milk

and a mug of tepid water,
and on my plate a newspaper
spread open at 'The Trillion Dollar Question'
(you had written 'keep this')
about the vast numbers,

the trillions and zillions.
To help Obama put his rescue plan, its full scale,
into perspective, it said, one trillion seconds
would take you back 31,709 years
to the time of the hunter-gatherers.

I tried to plot the story of your morning,
your movements and thoughts,
from these few things,
like an archaeologist puzzling
over pots and beakers.

Now I stare at Zurbarán's
'Cup of water and a rose on a silver plate',
the calm of the pale beaker, pared down,
at the centre of a shining dish,
the rose, pink and white, full blown,

beginning to droop, on its rim.
Around them darkness, the dull brown table.
No hands nearby; nothing to reveal
its place in the artist's life,
his habits, the story.

Dream Landings

1

They're washed in towards me
on a dark beery sea,
disappearing, appearing like

messages in bottles: Bowcher,
my uncle's old family chauffeur –
he's retired – can we arrange

a gathering to meet
at his house and give him
something to live for?

I hardly knew him.
And the small boy Pip
across the road

from the farm – something's
wrong, it's his heart.
He's perky to start with,

then frailer and frailer,
till we find him, a small creature,
 almost an insect, struggling out

onto the road, his crutches
like silver hatpins,
one with a broken knob.

And so many others washed in
on this sea, my anxiety seeping uselessly
into the water.

2

It was night-time.
We all crammed in, my sister
 and brother-in-law too, our friend,

small and hunched, holding tightly
to the steering wheel.
When we reached the ancient

mud-walled garden and saw
the great tulip tree, magnificent
in the greenish moonlight

we were intoxicated;
there were giant avocados
growing sideways

on the branches. We
looked more closely and
saw the avocados

were pigeons sleeping
in the moonlight.
We stared and stared.

3

After her funeral, when we each put
a flower on her woven coffin
and the farewells were so precise,

so moving, she came back again.
She was not a ghost,
she was there on the sofa.

Our wishing gave her eyes that
opened and shut. Her presence
was like a toy, a rabbit

or something we loved
with a stuffed pale body, given to us
long ago, held in sleep.

4

Sometimes you drag yourself up
from the waves, hair streaming,
or you can't quite get to the shore –

there's still a beat, a beat around you –
you're pulled back, pulled along
sideways, can't emerge.

But some days they flip you over,
the small waves, the softly
seething ones that nudge you

on to the pale sand – back
and forward, back and forward –
then wash you up, stranded

and soon almost forgetting
the world of floating where eyes
are level with a glittering field.

But it comes and goes – how
it was, how you're free of it and
how dry land is less familiar now.

Though Your Backs are Turned

for Fred and Grace

The white and silver estuary strung
    with black stakes at sunset, its watery skin
        drawing down the remaining light

from the sky, near where the cows are
    in silhouette on the horizon, very still now –
        you don't notice all this

through the window, where you're
    curled up on the floor writing comics
        and drawing huge flowers;

but will it be there later, somehow imprinted
    in you though your backs are turned,
        as a field half-seen from a speeding train –

a triangular field
    rusty red hemmed in by the boles
        of trees dark with ivy –

remains with me, or a book
    I half-read in glances and carry
        up and down stairs with me.

'Interior 1893' *

Nuque, nuca, nape –
    the soft domesticated *n*s of her neck,
        creamy, lit in sunlight coming from

a source we cannot see,
    her back to us where she sits
        reading perhaps a letter –

loose white blouse, soft hair,
    in *this colourful work*, says
        the catalogue, where so much colour

is carefully missing.
    There's no handle on
        the open door, no clues to her face,

her expression –
    a muted language of
        distance, avoidance, tenderness.

* A painting by the Danish artist, Vilhelm Hammershoi (1864–1916).
Many of his interiors show his wife turned away, her back to us.

Magnolia stellata

'You mustn't be afraid, dear Mother-in-law, that Vilhelm's paintings will become infected by the French.' – Ida, Hammershoi's wife

He's not intoxicated by her face
or distressed by it
or by a *Magnolia stellata*
in a garden,

white, white, white,
its torn petals
in the sun.

Instead the white door
gleams softly. It opens
on to another door
which is closed.

Pool of dimness. No clues
to her temperament,
her mood

ruffle the still apartment,
a clock ticking,
the slow growth of
something in his mind:

an indoor magnolia,
turned away, composed,
fine furniture enclosing her,

warding off violence,
violence of the red dancers
or an easel set up in a rut
in a field of flowers.

Your Blouse

for Valerie Clarke

Crisply made of white mussolino
   from Mosul in Mesopotamia,

your blouse with its tucks, its small
   flattened folds, narrowing us

down into a cool past, has a trim
   of las (lacere – to ensnare) –

those bands of delicate
   openwork fabric in wrought

and applied patterns, and
   botons – small knobs or studs

covered with that same mussolino
   or muslin, the word that

in our language was once slang
   for the fair sex; and sleeves,

neatly gadred at the shoulder,
   reaching to your elbows

and marked with straight
   creases from your hot iron.

My Dress with Vines

Remember how the colours went,
its huge vine-leaf wings and frogspawn eyes?

Bands of leaves, red black red black,
bold, orderly pairs of palms,

my mother's firm hands pressing me forward
farther than I wanted to go into the world

where a solid young man waited.
She asked him whether he liked the dress,

its neck that's called heart-shaped, its full skirt.
'Yes,' he said, and thought. 'It's vinous.'

A big dipper ride – 'Please open your eyes,' he begged.
The grape eyes were green with black circles

and dots, staring out of a bed of white,
as if she were anxiously keeping its eyes on me.

Do you grow into what your clothes are saying?
Is that why choosing was anguish always?

I wasn't into the preening and tumbling out
into the world of fun she wanted for me.

Instead the dress belonged to 'whoops', a *bal*
in the village of Vouziers, the champagne region,

and the stranger who asked me to dance –
I stuck, then tripped on his foot.

And it lasted like a flag, waving me through
my clumsy dancing years, out of step,

and she dancing beside me, still
tangling through me, outstripping me.

Remembering Elephants

A summer trying to remember elephants, how they visited
their dead, their laying on of trunks, how they fondled the tusks
of the dead, staying on and on. In my mind still seeing them,

oblivious in caravan, between the pillars of Kings Cross Station
and the rushed concrete of other dead places, as I trail
up and down England with my rucksack, my L.L. Bean bag,

like a student with a railcard and the mirage of family.
Those elephant ways of moving and thinking, how will I
hold on to them: the baby between the tree trunk legs,

the moving forest slowing down for him, the moving island
coming back for him, wickerwork of sun on
leathery backs, sun lighting up the baby's forehead

as they trample past villagers' houses, stripping trees
and tearing up bushes, lumbering steadily
and trumpeting their sorrow?

Vanishing Faces

for my Mother

Ambushed by notes,
those little notes he sends you,

your eldest grandson:
in the bottom of the sugar pot

'white sugar is very bad for our bodies',
and on your shopping list

'get organic'; and
a daughter's message

telling you to put a little oil
in the bath water

or the carer's, reminding you
what's there for lunch.

They are vanishing faces
and your mind brushes past them

like knee-high wet grass
in the early morning.

Glimmer

In this lane the fog comes down quickly,
its stiff army blanket muffling

what was bright a moment before,
your brooch on the dusty ground, wild

strawberries in the hedge still glimmering
but just behind you, nothing.

Paper Thin

The car's waiting. We are
the other side of the big unchanging space

of pale gravel chips. We call out to you –
are you all right?

Your face is intent on where
you're going, its folds

strong like crumpled white
paper. You hold your handbag

and walk forward
tenaciously

but seem to be moving
backwards into the dark pines.

Terre d'Acier

Compact, and demure as sprigged cotton,
this casserole, disinterred from
a French garden, a spray of blue leaves

neatly tucked under each scrolled handle,
came from my mother – she dug it up
in a flowerbed, on holiday

in the Dordogne with her best friend
Helen. Look at the band
of blue pinks round the rim,

the gently shelving-in base,
a faint beading above the angle,
a small blemish in the glaze

where grey clay shows through
like a birthmark; plain inside,
the glaze like thin cream. On its base

is a blurred monogram and
her message of endurance,
the hard-to-read words TERRE D'ACIER.

From the Terrace

for my sister Judy

Why is it painful, this
calm landscape:
black shadows of cypresses

on the pink earth
of the vineyard, the tidied
stakes and wires,

vines hardly begun, the poplars
just starting to have a haze,
and on the foothills

of the Luberon
the distant green
fuzz of new things

like an effort of the land
to get up and
start all over again?

Provence

The lavender ball, the bag of juniper shavings: 'Press them, squeeze them,
they will last for five or even ten years,' said the market stallholder.

It's May. We hear the cuckoo on our walk
up the valley towards the cedar forest.
The bell-like call seems to still the day,
still it to a white path along the edge
of a field of flowers. The village clock strikes
each half hour, then again for workers
in the fields who didn't hear it the first time;
at night too, its loud melodious bell.
I lean over the edge of the terrace,
peer at the smallholding far below,

wondering why each row of vines is finished
with a white rose bush; why the cypresses
have been planted in close pairs,
small dark fingers repeated over and over
on the hillside; why the lime trees are clipped
in box shapes. I long for the house
with its thumb of a tower, growing out of
a harmonious jumble of grey-green
olive trees which remind me of
the wall paintings of Livia's garden.

It's hot in the forest. We leave the path,
looking for an open view to the south.
Horse droppings; churned up patches
of earth made by wild boar. Once a boar
with her file of striped ginger babies
ran across our path and scrambled up
into the wood. The friendly cyclists
appear and reappear, walking
this time in their shiny cycling gear.
'How small we are', says the wife.

In the evening the wind gets up
and blows through our conversations.
We watch the windy sunset. The sky is sliced
in a strange diagonal formation: on one side,
streaks of sunset, on the other, black cloud
down to the horizon, the zones divided by
a straight edge. At night we pull the heavy
blue cover over the pool, shutting in things
we have brought with us, our family clouds,
closing them down in the glittering blue.

Homecoming

Is there a heavy tree there
or a poplar like water
running, glistening,

or is it somewhere I can reach out to
very early in the morning
when the light is still deep

and the low sun begins to bake
into the brick wall opposite,
or is it a tawny hillside

where great footprints of rock
I stare at seem to come towards me
steadily? Not one place but any

where I stop and wait
as if for the homecoming
of a distant father.

Ice Sculpture

in memory of my Father

The slow eerie performance of ice language:
people with bare arms stare in the heat,
wait. It drips and slushes in the park
through the hot day.

The wall of ice blocks, upstanding and distant,
ice face glimmering with someone's
most heartfelt junk frozen inside it,
face of great ice blooms, of shapes

like frost-misted cabbages under glass,
grainy Christmas trees and a locked-away
figure stooping in a snowstorm
melt down, opening out

to the green beyond, taking us
with shudders and crashes to an ice heap
where his tumbled things fall out
like toys, fresh and small.

Ice face, Father, your world moved into
frosted glass – until the laying bare, the splintering,
the jutting out round the edges of your real things,
things I can reach in the rubble of ice –

the runner-bean flower buttonhole
from your impromptu wedding, your owl spectacles,
your Brahms Lieder in a blue binding, the Cornish dainties
she sent up to you after war broke out,

your anxious love letters, their broken story;
and your ashes, scattered not on some vague
Welsh mountainside, but in the kitchen garden
of your sister's house by the river at Glyn Ceiriog.

After the ice sculpture 'A fresh bunch of flowers', in memory of Stephen Cripps
by Anne Bean, Paul Burwell and Richard Wilson, in Hyde Park, 1992.

Setting Sail

for Christophe and Kate

In spite of the clear of everything in its place,
    jars labelled in black felt pen,

a new log opened, the knot school,
    an oar repaired again –

in spite of the gasket at last flown in
    from Athens, rope circles

on deck like giant bleached ammonites,
    insurance debates, confabulations

striving to be empty of everything
    but careful planning –

in spite of the Yamaha outboard motor
    at last joined together

in holy gasketry, the tight white
    of the ship's world –

in the galley, a green swatch of dill,
    two halves of garlic clove

and a bottle top make an accidental
    cartoon creature, and

brains exhausted with judgment
    skip the weather forecast

and are flooded with let's go, let's go –
    off into the gale.

Porthole

for David

What is left (all bickering, all
power talk of gaskets drained away)?
Just three small figures in a rubber
dinghy, two bonded together,

the thin and the square,
each with an oar
rowing silently, and you
leaning back stiffly smiling

in your silly blue and black
French curate's sunhat;
and on the terrace of
Fish Restaurant Beautiful Alice,

someone standing up,
staring out to sea,
moving across the terrace
and sitting down again

above the yellow wood balustrade
and rivers of green creeper
whose magenta flowers
open to the sun and close

in tight twists as the light goes;
and the faces of three swimmers
always beating towards the boat,
shouting silently and smiling.

Alikes Bay, Thassos 1995

Honeysuckle

for Grace

Secretly at first through
   dark green discs of leaves
      small tongues stretch out,

then under cover open
   into winged flowers,
      white tinged with red,

still sheltered in tangled
   brown and green.
      The scent comes then –

sweet, peppery, drifting through,
   in and out of the kitchen,
      almost reluctant, like you –

you, starting in darkness
   and then here, quiet at first
      as if away in another room,

lying stolid with your pointed lips,
   your small purple legs, your still
      blood-streaked head and nose.

Walking in the Garden with Fred

When the fuchsia showers its thousands
of drooping pink lips towards you

and your closed eyes blink and twitches
of new expressions work across your face

as we bravely walk out
into the unimaginably white light

when the rain's stopped and it seems that
everything in the garden is shivering

and nosing up or making small bounces
like spasms of undirected legs and arms,

I think, if we take a new pink thing
into a room, we see all the other pinks

already there, and how the place is full of them
though for a long time we haven't noticed.

White Flags

for Ramy

Precisely, delicately
you take a tissue, just one,
from the box by the bed

and race with it,
your small white flag,
up up the garden stairs

into the kitchen
and put it carefully
in the wastepaper basket,

then hurry down for
the next one – and the next –
intent, not seeing us.

We look down
into the green garden
laughing and think

it's mimicking,
it has another meaning,
it's missing the point,

and you slip through
our hands as the wind
riffles through the new

leaves on the trees here,
through the translucent
copper-pink leaves.

Wildebeest

The whistle then pause of his snore
    was for an instant the cry

of a newborn in the next room
    or a small owl's distant whoop

way beyond the downs of their bed.
    Half-waking, she saw again the birth

of a wildebeest – the silver and red
    scarf of its afterbirth streaming out,

how it floundered and collapsed,
    then staggered up again, soon

unfolding and running with its mother –
    filmed from every angle using hippo-cam,

dragonfly-cam, tortoise-cam, croc-cam.
    And she thought of the child

they might have had, bounding across
    their wordless bridge, so full

of blood, consuming the space,
    but all in silence, no close-up

of the sounds of being born and
    giving birth, no feeling of

the senses running and flowing
    in danger like the wildebeest.

Painted Wooden Boat, Egyptian

'I'll follow those birds,
   the just-touching-the-water
      blue wings that know

the skimming way.
   They carefully hold
      the still ant's egg,

the seeds
   in their little pods,
      trail, flick their wings

and then point up
   again their sapphire heads –
      easy, deft, touch

of orange – as if,
   "I'll catch these first, dive
      under that branch,

then forward on
   the turquoise sheen."
      I know it's death, carrying

my serious burden,
   but balance-magic,
      the tree pose on water

will speed us to Abydos
   undisturbed.'

But She is Not Sailing Anywhere

For the seventh birthday celebration
   you settle your model sampan
      in the small garden pond,

lean, pointed, made for speed,
   a painted eye on the prow
      looking forward –

among the reeds and irises
   it fills most of the space.
      And you put the Japanese doll

into the sampan on her red cushion,
   gaudy and stolid,
      in her bright kimono.

I write in my notebook
   'landlocked Japanese princess
      in a sampan', thinking

landlocked a good word
   for the princess sitting in her boat
      going nowhere, as surely as

I shall never sail to Japan where
   Basho set off on his lonely journeys,
      his windswept spirit

not finding peace with itself
   since he began writing poetry
      and became a wanderer.

And I wonder if the Japanese princess
   would have pitied him as she sits
      secure, in her red and gold kimono.

Miniature

Radha is chasing a shadow,
the shadow of a kite,
distant, elusive,

with suppleness and grace –
the curve of her body, her dress
of pale blackberry.

With one hand she holds back
her green-lined veil as she
swoops down towards

the two-winged shadow. It is
pencil grey: she almost touches it.
The wall behind her is pink.

In the top left-hand corner
the diminutive Krishna –
his blue skin, his yellow costume –

is flying the kite. It is about
separation, only shadow
in this shadowless world.

For Howard Fussiner

Howard, those summers,
every morning early
you walked up the curved path

round the edge of the field
alone, to your miniature studio
in the top left-hand corner.

I think of you and I think of
colour: emerald green
mountains, sandy rocks,

pine-tufted islands and
indigo sea of the Maine coast –
you were reaching out

again and again as if
you still had not caught them,
searching, miles away,

in your studio shed
on the edge of
the pine wood.

Unpeopled Morning

The trees suck me out of bed
    at five in the morning. I stare deep

into the eyeless trees, their colourless
    velvet, their gustiness speaking only tree.

I'm absent from the sky, the vibrating
    cool of deep blue and monochrome

of the hills, the lightening darkness
    before dawn where the trees have taken over again,

blotting us out, and the rooster begins talking
    rooster through his unseen scrawny neck.

I can rest in these spaces
    which carry on without us, our gestures,

our interferences, without our language
    lying on the land; and when early morning air

creeps in through gaps in the door
    how could I ever name its white scents?

Tree House

The shining room floats
   in the dark trees.

My white cupboard is there,
   the small indoor pastel

of trees on my white wall,
   the edge of the kitchen table,

the fruit bowl.
   The calathea plant's striped leaves

on a high shelf are also
   in my neighbour's lighted window.

My white door opens
   into the neighbour's house.

The room is suspended in the black
   tossing roaring trees.

It is clear-edged, its welcome is steady.
   But as I move towards the window

to look into my bright room,
   I already know it will slide away

into shadow, pitch-dark,
   wind-blown, full of leaves.

Deep Forest

for Christophe

When you said 'Are we going into the unknown?
I'm very familiar with it', I laughed.
We laughed together but I wrote your words

on a small piece of paper
and they merged with something I had just read
about coming

> *to the borders of sleep,*
> *The unfathomable deep*
> *Forest where all must lose*
> *Their way ...*

I wonder how you can live so intimate with the unknown,
so close it becomes like your tweed jacket and peaked cap, your small cigar,
which will all become strange, unworded, one day,

or like your family, your familiars: who are those
backs of men sitting at my table, who don't speak to me,
don't seem to know me, make me invisible in my own house?

Things become half-worded, like the packet of camel mile:
'Difficult to fit in a cupboard, a mile of camels',
you joke, and mean the puzzlement too.

I know it in glimpses – a black and white jacket,
but the face drops away, or a scent lingers beside me but
a name has gone. The deep forest brushes past, comes nearer –

close as the stranger in the hospital bed beside mine
whose daughters stood around her all night
like dark waiting trees.

The lines in italics are from Edward Thomas's 'Lights Out.'

The Shingle Bank

We sat there, the three of us,
   above the falling away, sudden and steep,
to the sea. At our backs, down below,
   spread ordinary land,

the scenery of flat fields, drainage dykes,
   thistles, black and white cows,
the necessary church tower
   from panoramas in childhood books.

You were so lost that weekend –
   your clothes went on strangely,
you came out for breakfast,
   a nightdress over your T-shirt and

I struggled to put your second arm
   into the sleeve of your buttoned-up jacket,
feeling your fury. You took off
   in slanting directions,

a confusing magnet dragging you.
   But when we came to this edge
there was nowhere else to go.
   The vastness quietened you,

and the close pebbles –
   mottled, sandy, egg-shaped,
pocked, black – drew you
   into another vastness of detail.

You bedded down like a child
   and I took off to the release of
the thudding, grey-green water,
   a faraway seal's head bobbing.

*'But there will never be a revolution
in Russia.'* – Anton Chekhov

The corset and the bustle,
 a good hour of conversation,
her self-recrimination
that crept into your story,
the look a lady wears after –
a far cry from French novels.

You stare, fisher, into the teeming river,
wait with tackle and baskets,
and go down into the ravine,
tell how it is, the lives there
away from drawing rooms
in the sour corrupted village:

the sister-in-law with her small head,
unblinking eyes *like a viper peering
out of the spring rye*, in a rage
grabs a ladle of boiling water
and throws it over the baby,
the impotence of the mother –

you know the truth of these stories.
Injustices, nightingales, frogs, bitterns,
sky like a blanket of purple and gold brocade.
The sap of what you write is compassion,
or is it consolation? *The river is broad, deep
and beautiful. There are the following fish in it . . .*

City

'In times of crisis, we must all decide again and again whom we love.'
Frank O'Hara, To the Film Industry in Crisis

Bright heads bowl along the top of the privet hedge – magenta, blond –
their voices coming from the underworld of the privet –
in front, behind or somewhere else nearby; and across the road,
between half-opened shutters, the toy monkey hangs over
the back of the sofa again – a no-language message, 'I'm in' gesture?
In the neighbour's window, straw bird's-nests have replaced
the tortoiseshell cat children believed was real, but no, always
in the same place, its back to us. They are invisible, those who come
at night to lift up the great flowerpots and smash them in the dark.

What would *you* say to the city's night-time foxes, you who lived
in silver instants, sending love to . . . *the extras / who pass quickly
and return in dreams saying your one or two lines?* What do I say
to the extras I meet in bright encounters: the girl with her camera
at the bus shelter peering at a near-invisible spider's web –
'it's perfect', the man who sells me half a bunch of parsley,
saying 'in a democracy anything is possible'?
Bound to the city, mistrusting its broken images, I cannot ride
with its glittering momentary loves, like yours for the silver screen,
still casting about for the heavy words 'native of'.

Oranges

Once they were rare,
    found on a tarry beach in wartime
or heavy in stocking toes

at Christmas; eaten in the bath
    by an aunt privately
avoiding mess. We knew

all the ways of opening them
    to reach the golden ball of huddling pigs.
We turned the skins inside out

so our teeth could scrape off
    the last frayed juicy bits,
best of all if they were blood.

We hardly imagined orange trees,
    ungainly, overloaded,
humming with black bees –

and I'm still not ready
    for this abundance, this waste,
the scent of orange on my fingers,

all seasons here at once –
    fruiting, five-pointed flowers,
waxy young green leaves,

the older darker ones,
    drifts of windfall oranges, too many
to count, on the dry earth.

I stand near the glow, and then
    breathe in the glow, the geniality
that comes from more-than-enough –

yet feel a slight recoil, a wanting
    to hoard, hold back for the future,
ungenerous to myself.

The Wind Today

has blown away thoughts of oranges, the sense
    of oasis and trickling water. It's blown past our window
      a bent hurrying shape in a dark suit.

The Spanish wind blows woodsmoke
    and I remember burning peat in a Donegal summer, waiting
      for a quick blue sky to release

children onto the strand, shivering and legging around
    with mottled sandy skin. A bit later
      you come in. 'It's soft and warm', you say.

The bonfire smoke on the hill above
    is swirling gently now. The raucous frogs,
      sparrows, syncopated hammers are loud again.

Donegal stays too, in the bare lanes and pared down life
    where I've allowed a space in my mind,
      and the past smokes through.

Almàssera Vella, Alicante

Music of the hoboys is under the stage

Antony and Cleopatra, 1V iii

Lying there for months now,
the open book under my window
has been gathering yellow like pale sand,

offering up the words that won't quite leave,
that insist on their images:
Hark!

      Music i' th'air.

              Under the earth.

Outside, the bay tree is dying – its curling brown leaves –
and the autumn trees are stripped in wet winds.
Before, a bright moment of flare.

Plaintive, reedy music under the stage, as if
an unseen procession is passing, gauzy clothes billowing out –

'Tis the god Hercules, whom Antony lov'd,
Now leaves him.

Verandah

for David

What's the word? I've lost it, we keep saying. But
as we walk back to the Hotel Esperides in the dark,

a few lights shining in the empty street, globes
of light spaced along the edge of the olive grove,

you remember when you were a small boy in India and
your parents had gone out (perhaps your younger brother

was asleep already and your ayah didn't talk to you).
You'd lie in the heat under wet sheets and watch

the lights of planes landing in the distance at Chaklala Airbase
and imagine the bustle of pilots and crew on the tarmac

was just outside your window. Then you'd pretend
the verandah was a station platform, brightly lit,

and you were watching crowds of people, the great steam trains
coming in and out, and you'd feel part of it, less lonely.

You tell me this as we trudge up to the Esperides
with its sleeping people, its screen of palms,

as if you're still holding a lighted fishbowl full of
steam trains and crowds and pilots and wordless images,

carrying it intact up the dark road among the other
globes of light that have opened your memory.